Prisoner Projects Communication Teams

Communications Can Change Lives

Reverend Mike Wanner

Table of Contents

Table of Contents.. 3

Introduction.. 4

1 - What I have Already Written.. 5

2 - Why I am Writing This Book 6

3 - Where to Start? 7

4 - The Prison Community... 8

5 - Reasons for Testing 9

6 - Communication Planning 10

7 - Understanding Takes Time... 11

8 - The Best For All The Prisoners 12

9 - The Best For All The Prison Staff................................... 13

10 - The Best For Prisoners' Families 15

11 - The Best For All The Prison Staff & Their Families 18

12 - The Best For The Taxpayers 20

13 - Rotating Communication Priorities 21

14 - Spiraling Right.. 23

15 - Summary So Far 24

16 - Your Team Could Consider... 25

17 - Thank You 28

18 - Don't Worry Ever.. 29

19 - Resource Books 30

20 - Angels Please Prayers... 32

21 - Private Channeling 33

22 - Reverend Mike Wanner... 34

Introduction

These Books are to highlight the importance of ideas for new programs, new plans, new participation and new possibilities. Suffice it to say that we need a lot to change for 2.3 million residents of prisons to be able to find the motivation necessary to participate in improving their lives.

Little will change when the minds lack stimulation. On almost every issue, robust listening is full with the speaker's thinking that someone else needs to do something different.

I can tell you from my experience in life that the most important step is to try. I have read how scary prison can be and how hard it is to deal with all the inconvenience and stress. I have the freedom to express views that might help somewhat.

If you like the ideas I share, then consider developing the ideas further to spotlight what you can do. If you do not feel right with my suggestions, you can stay with what you know and develop your internal skills.

If you want things to be different, you need to take charge of all possibilities that you see to help each potential attract momentum.

There are people in prison who do not want to be there, and there are people outside who want to keep as many people as possible in jail. Unfortunately, a lot of individuals in prison can cause problems which turn in to a situation where their incarceration is extended, and that is not great.

1 - What I have Already Written

I started channeling Angel Raphael in 2013 and have written a series of books called Angel Raphael Speaks which evolved for me to publish the following books related to prisons:

1. *Angel Raphael Speaks Volume 4: Angels, Addicts, Alcoholics & Prisoners – Oh Yeah!*
2. *Angel Raphael Speaks Volume 5:* Prisoners Caring for Alcoholics - Australia In Miniature Projects Intro
3. *Angel Raphael Speaks Volume 6:* Prisoners Caring for Addicts - Australia In Miniature For Addicts
4. *Prison Jobs Now: Providing Care For Addicts And Alcoholics*
5. *Angel Raphael Speaks - Prisons* (A Kindle only book -2013)
6. *Contained Care Communities Concept*
7. *Australia In Miniature*
8. *Prison Possibilities Dialogue Series: Concept*
9. *Prison Possibilities Dialogue Series: Volume 2 Dialogues*
10. *Prison Possibilities Dialogue Series: Volume 3 Dialogues*
11. *Prison Possibilities Dialogue Series: Volume 4 Dialogues*
12. *Prison Possibilities Dialogue Series: Volume 5 Dialogues*
13. *Prison Possibilities Voluntary Exile: Concept*
14. *Prison Possibilities Correction Coaches: Concept*
15. *Prison Possibilities for Mexicans: Is A Boat Better than A Wall?*
16. *Prison Possibilities Family Time: A Reason to Thrive!*
17. Prison Genius Pool: "So Much Genius In Jail"
18. *Prison Possibilities Access Systems: Prisoner Access by Request*
19. *Prisoner's Lawyers Can Save The American Economy: Make A Buck Doing It & Be Thanked!*
20. *Prisoner Family Talks, Days, Stays & Vacations: Connecting Helps Healing*
21. *Prisoner Writing Projects: Write To Heal, Start Over & Reconnect*
22. *Prison Cell Clearing & Blessing: Clear Entities, Chase Ghosts, and & Create Sacred Space*
23. *Prisoner Professors*
24. *Prison Reiki? Maybe Someday? A Gateway To Help Heal Prisons & America?*
25. *Judges And An Angel Rule On Possibilities: We Can Cut Sentences & Prison Costs*
26. *Ideas For Prison Wardens: Leadership Is Not Easy*
27. *Solitary Community: Could Community Support Cut Costs and Issues?*

2 - Why I am Writing This Book

Prison may have suppressed the joy that you once had and the separation can leave you feeling hopeless but working towards a goal can help.

Restoring purpose to one's life can be motivational. The options to do that may be small, but open minds can think things through and create possibilities, plans, projects and team efforts to work toward mutual goals.

I read a lot and write a lot and listen a lot. Reading can be helpful to share focus and learn about potentials. I read a lot because understanding better is a progressive goal of my existence.

I write a lot because that can be an effective way to share ideas that might ignite the flame of possibility in another so they can capture a concept that I wish to share. Writing saves me from repeating myself forever to people who might tune the ideas out. We all have only a little time, and I feel writing helps me reach more people quicker. So far, I Have given away many thousands of my books.

I listen a lot to those who feel that they are stuck and there are no possibilities for better days. It saddens me when I hear the depressing dialogue that so many say so often because when - They focus on limitation, They Create More.

My Recommendation Would Be to Focus on Optimism and Create More!

3 - Where to Start?

The first step would be a preliminary evaluation to determine your expectations about a level of receptivity and openness that you might expect from the facility that is holding you.

You need to be diligent and revisit the rules about your responsibilities as a resident. It would be wise to consider if you are allowed to communicate and how.

There are thousands of different dedicated incarceration facilities in America alone, and each may offer you precise problems and opportunities. It could be a lot easier to participate in efforts that are moving in a similar direction as you wish to go instead of starting a new discussion.

The path of least resistance could be a wise goal for your concept consideration. Accessing and complying with the local rules could be the most important part of your efforts in the early days.

Administrators of the world, in general, are usually most receptive to creativity when it is served up in a way that complies with the **exact** specifications of the rules of their particular authority as granted by their superiors. That path makes it easier for them to move forward with worthy projects without bias claims from others seeking attention.

A smooth path can avoid potholes that derail journeys of possibility. Potholes could cause things to shift to not now and then maybe not ever.

4 - The Prison Community

The prison community has unique dynamics, and each person acts in ways that may sometimes seem mysterious. Please know that the behavior in a closed community can be somewhat predictable but not always.

What you send out via your energy and interaction with the community will blend with many other efforts and influence the big picture. When everybody is miserable in an organization, misery abounds.

When upliftment occurs, it influences those taking it in and many times; higher vibration energy can change lives. There will be no benefit for down and out prisoners to try a halfway effort.

Patience is a virtue, so it will serve you well if you embrace it. Will You?

The community includes everybody so listen up and spread your awareness to include all that you like and all that may present challenges for you. Before you can invite others to your discussion, you need to put your head on straight.

Test yourself for readiness, can you:
1. Consider What is Best For All The Prisoners?
2. Consider What is Best For All The Prison Staff?
3. Consider What is Best For All The Prisoners' Families?
4. Consider What is Best For All The Prison Staff Families?
5. Consider What is Best For All The Taxpayers?

5 - Reasons for Testing

The challenges of openness and sensitivity that I mentioned will be very significant to your analysis and planning because a bad start could wreck the possibilities. Best to start right or not at all.

Disconnection seems to be very pivotal to the feelings of self-worth and the ability to get along with people. Prisoners can feel that they are permanently labeled when convicted of a crime, and the public identity can also be internalized and make things more difficult.

The testing of team building can be a potential tool for you to test yourself and your team to see if you are ready to work with each other and rebuild your lives. It may sound simple, but there seems to be a disconnection of many things for prisoners that can be too personal or too revealing.

Those small disconnects may be part of a larger problem that may make societal reconnection involved. While one is in prison, life goes on in the isolation that is so natural, but that will not help when you are trying to reconnect with others later so expanding your understanding of others before you exit can help.

Team building could assist those who want to prepare for success outside the walls.

Little steps early on can make freedom less stressful and provide a head start to confidence.

6 - Communication Planning

Remember all the readiness test categories of community members and then invite each potential member to speak to their willingness to diligently look at the facility's policies and reflect on their ability to participate in a team effort. Decide how much time it will take to allow each team member candidate enough time to do that homework.

Next step would be to schedule a second meeting where everyone can report back with their recommendations for a plan. The committee would have to be a reasonable size to be approved by prison officials.

Evaluation of the proposals would need to be diligent enough to satisfy administration that the effort has integrity and value.

Families and Taxpayers are Pivotal

The inclusion of Prisoner's families and Prison Staff families and Taxpayer families are pivotal to a revitalization of options for the prisoners' lives and their projects.

Consideration and respect for all are characteristics that we all can get used to because what comes around goes around and those attributes are desirable for us all. In other words, if a wave of love is desired all around then a wave of respect and consideration needs to be started by the one who desires the goal so that the basic gestures are reciprocated and magnified by all who appreciate the spark of dignity sought and shared.

7 - Understanding Takes Time

There is great power in listening. When you hear the words team members select, you can have an insight into the way they think and how well they deal with obstacles that come up.

Communication and understanding seem to have the greatest benefit when all participants feel the willingness to participate. Belonging to any group can have some satisfaction, but it may also offer some perspective that is unfamiliar. Please relax into the values that you collectively choose to serve all the interests.

I would encourage teams to work together to understand changes and how that can influence different people differently. Openness and sensitivity may seem to present challenges for prisoners as those characteristics might be weak and vulnerable but when you get out your audience will be different, and the new audience will be important to your success.

Sensitivity could be that proverbial blessing or curse, so the exercise of caution, preciseness, diligence and the selective application will be key to your success or failure.

Mutual goals and support will be more likely if you can bond to a special level with members of your team so that they can support one another. It may seem hard to achieve in prison, so I caution all to take your time team building because that bond can make your success more likely.

8 - The Best For All The Prisoners

Families can surround members with love and support. Prisons are not as helpful.

Bridging the gap between the two situations can help prisoners tolerate the day to day grind. Easier said than done but that is true of all things.

Please do not expect this to be an easy task as the experiences of each prisoner can be very different. Just because you can identify with a person does not mean that you can understand their struggle or know how to help them.

Progress can be made in little steps at the beginning of an effort and then gain momentum as people get to know, understand and trust each other. Listening can help healing and willingness to share can help self-confidence.

There is a part of human nature that wants to share knowledge with others. Many prisoners have been through a lot of experiences in their lives. They may not be quick to open up to someone that they met recently.

Patience with others can help participants to offer it to themselves in ways they would never have thought. Hearing others ask for help also may help some to ask for it themselves.

Forming a group of your peers is very helpful to build confidence and find support or at least someone to talk with from time to time.

9 - The Best For All The Prison Staff

Being less than cooperative with prison staff may seem very logical. When one fills any kind or role in life, there are things that come with that position that may feel good or not so good.

Your team building exercises can extend to the prison staff in a way that is not patronizing or confrontational. Yesterday is no more, but the association of positional interaction can stay as good or bad as ever or reach new highs or new lows.

You cannot choose the behavior of other prisoners or the prison staff. You can choose your behavior, and you can change your behavior in many ways.

There is no way to expect that one action by you of anybody on your team will generate a significant change in an action by other prisoners or prison staff. There are many human dynamics in your facility, and only you can determine the complexity and reactions that might be triggered if you are not careful.

If your team can determine reasonable efforts that the larger population can embrace which publicly show some effort towards cooperative goal setting, then clear messages can be offered to the staff and administration and eventually the larger community.

The energy in prison may not be to your liking, but all who occupy space within the walls contribute to the energy that exists there. Positive change does not happen without efforts by a lot of people.

All who want positive change can contribute to its creation by being as positive as possible for as long as possible. Everybody impacts the prison staff, and when things go right for them, they can share their positivity, and that can make many days go a lot smoother.

The efforts that you team considers to suggest will likely be best directed to the whole prison staff community and not to particular staffers.

There is a way to say and do everything that helps to deliver messages in a way that they are most likely to succeed. For team building and interactions with staff, a professional demeanor lacking any sly implications or subtle digs could be your best option.

A part of team building is to embrace the best characteristics that everybody in the group has to offer and then use their best to create a message that is helpful to all collectively.

A good interaction can lead to more and then hopefully more candid and beneficial understanding that can take the edge off interactions in the future.

10 - The Best For Prisoners' Families

Family members are important to many prisoners, and each can be key to help some prisoners recreate their family connections and then their societal connections.

I have written two other books about family connectivity but the key to all that is communication. Of course, communication is a big problem for prisoners because of all the impediments and cost of communication.

I would hope that your communication team can develop efficient connections through third-party Pro Bono organizations who can funnel meaningful continuous communication. I think E-cards and Message Codes and perhaps Scripture References can help convey feelings. Creativity can also help to develop more tools that could be concise but meaningful.

Efforts that are transparent are more likely to pass security scrutiny and be able to keep the relationships from being dormant. Just being remembered can make a big difference on both sides of the walls.

On the next two pages of this Chapter, I will paste two references to the importance of communication.

The First is from Prison Possibilities Family Time and the second from Prison Possibilities Dialogue Series: Volume 4 Dialogues.

Communication & Continuation Of Love

Continuation of the feeling of being loved is most difficult when the communication of that love is stifled by the restrictions of the facilities that contain the one incarcerated. While the officials may feel with some reported justification that security challenges are presented with communication, I am hopeful that we can somehow find a middle position that provides the level of security needed by facilities that also allows some love communications that are needed by the families.

I pray that there can be sometimes be an acceptable level of standardized communication that therefore needs less restriction that can be created to bi-laterally meet some more of the needs of institutions and families so that more bits of love can be transmitted and received on both sides of the wall.

To that end, I have previously written in my Dialogue series books an idea that might help. I have posted that idea below for your reference in the same style as it resides in the book.

{From:
Prison Possibilities Dialogue Series: Volume 4 Dialogues}

Presenting

PPDS Message Codes?

Communication seems to be such a challenge for prisoners and their families, so I wanted to float an idea about sending brief publicly available message codes to expedite a simple note.

A= all	A2= and	A3=as	A4= ARE
B= be	B2= best	B3= but	
C= can	C2= could		
D= do	D2= dear	D3=did	
E= I love my spouse			
F= for	F2=find		
G= good			
H= hi	H2=have	H3=how	
I=I	I2=if	I3=it	
J=just			
K=know			
L= let	L2=location	L3=last	
M= my	M2=maybe		
N= no	N2=not	N3=need	
O=ok			
P= please	P2=page		
Q=I love my child/children			
R=rent	R2=re		
S= so	S2=she		
T= the	T2=thank T3=thanks		
U=you			
V=very			
W= we	W2=what W3=when		
X=thinking of you			
Y=you	Y2=yes		
$=money			
!=important			
@= a location			
#=number			
%=percentage			
&=and			

Examples:

"E Q H3 A4 U" = "I love my spouse, I love My Children. How are you?"

"I N3 $" = "I need money."

Comments and code suggestions invited. Thanks.

11 - The Best For All The Prison Staff & Their Families

Prison Staff will probably have very different priorities than prisoners. Communication teams may start with the consideration of the values that staff members and their families hold dear.

High on the list, one may expect to find safety and career advancement. Staff members might be interested in hearing about those topics.

Both the topics can mutually serve both the prison staff and the prisoners. Peaceful prisons can help safety be the norm for all.

Of course, Peace can be elusive, but goal setting can help to maximize the potential for peace. Goals can be set by communicating priorities and weighing the values that are important to all who occupy space within the walls as residents or staff.

Again, communication is the tool of choice so that physical struggles and confrontations can be avoided. Communication teams can discuss both sides of all potential topics so that understanding can be factored into all decisions.

Understanding takes time, and role playing in communication teams can be a very effective tool for prisoners to use so that can happen. Those Prisoners who play the role of prison staff may be thoroughly enlightened by the issues that come up of which they have never previously considered.

Career enhancement also is an area that prison staff interest may help the prisoner situation. One of the areas that I wrote about is called Corrections Coaches which I believe is non-existent but could be pivotal to the development of prisoner rehabilitation.

Motivated corrections coaches could change everything for everybody. The status quo in most prisons does not seem to be very encouraging for anybody, but understanding can be very intriguing.

Corrections Coaches could be instrumental in aligning prisoners with potentials that they may never have been in a position to consider. If given an opportunity and a way to do it, I believe that many corrections officers would find the ability to help a prisoner grow and step up the rehabilitation ladder toward many of the benefits that positivity could have.

If there could be a more neutral setting for understanding and kindness without effort, I believe that human nature could allow circumstances of healing understanding.

12 - The Best For The Taxpayers

Taxpayers have an important interest in everything that goes on in prison, but the complexity of the system keeps them from knowing too much. Taxpayers pay the bills, and the cost is huge.

Taxpayers lives are diminished by the huge cost of prisons that take funds from the common pool that exists to benefit the whole of the country. Providing the best for all the taxpayers will involve minimizing the costs to the lowest level necessary to provide for the safety of the greater community.

Part of the work for the communication team could well be to provide outreach to the taxpayers in a way they can be understand while they are not knowledgeable about the complexity of the system that incarcerates so many for so long.

Taxpayers need to see a simpler interpretation of things. Communication would not be easy but could happen over time if there evolve some basic views of low-cost options which could provide highly efficient options for the facilities, the communities and the prisoners.

13 - Rotating Communication Priorities

The communications team can be successful by creating a series of projects on which to focus. Your significant understanding will come when you take on the persona of those who you are to focus on and then realize that their priorities are interactive with yours.

As you begin to see how one thing interacts with another, your team understanding of the other's needs will be enhanced. Next, will be your team understanding of the interactive modifications that will be needed to have the priorities tweaked enough to raise the compatibility of each proposal that your team offers others.

Documenting understanding will allow others to see your team growth of comprehension so that they can see the reality of your team's new comprehension and how they might be able to build upon that comprehension to further communicate the things that they want you to know.

While it may seem quite awkward for your team to speak the new understanding of what others may see you share, it also allows you to choose words that are most likely to be compatible with the reader's point of view and motivations while still being acceptable to those who chose you to represent them.

To practice interactive awareness, role playing assignments for different members of your team can allow them to react quickly to what they perceive to be the way that the real role person they represent would react.

Prisoners represented can feel the precise nature of your words and how they align to be most compatible for all involved.

Before you share anything tough outside your team, consider sharing role player' reactions in a role negotiation that might someday be usable in a real negotiation.

As a team, consider taking a series of topics for consideration and then assigning perspective positions to different individuals so they can get some sense of reality check as if the discussion was real.

Perhaps early on you could pick three topics and then run them through a series of discussions having each role player participate as if real.

Your role players would anchor the perspectives of:

> 1. The Prisoners
> 2. The Prison Staff
> 3. The Prisoners Families
> 4. The Prison Staff Families
> 5. The Taxpayers

As you develop your process, some situations could be benefitted by dropping the Families categories and maybe adding:

> 1. Wardens or Other Supervisors
> 2. Government Agency Directors as appropriate for your Jurisdiction.

14 - Spiraling Right

Have you ever listening to self-centered People where they talk about their view of the world as it relates to things that they are the only one interested in as the topics are self-serving and self-flattering.

When listening to people like that, have you ever examined how you feel about what you are hearing? You might notice that you are feeling uneasy about the value of their message.

Many times, you might notice that you are resistant to their message as they have not connected with you because their message is about them. In this communication team process, I invite you not to be like them because self-centeredness will not be helpful to the dynamic that will serve the most people. They are spiraling down toward isolation and self-interest.

I invite all readers to consider that giving and receiving can be the same under the right circumstances. For me, the best foot forward is always a step in the right direction.

Little courtesies can evolve to shifts in possibilities and the potential for all. Helpful in that pursuit can be very easy and minor efforts toward positivity.

Readers are cautioned that these comments do not invite unreasonable expectations of exuberant effects that border on a lottery win. The effects will be subtle and cumulative over time, but each very simple baby step can be monumental over time in recreating a new view of what is, was and can be. Positivity and connectedness can help you to spiral up to God & Community.

15 - Summary So Far

The prison situation is not going to change overnight but the quality of life for each prisoner can.

You can change the impact of things that exist in the now and the future. It takes time.

Building a house can take time, but it is well worth the effort. Houses do not have as many obstacles to construction as prisons have to change.

If you are getting impatient already, I invite you to let go of that because it will probably not serve you. I am talking a slow process, but to succeed, you must start.

You must decide for yourself if you will listen at all to what I have written and you must also decide whether to risk change. The risks that you face in your particular situation are unknown to me, and I cannot help you there.

Within your head, may be a great powerhouse of potential if you do everything within your power to stay in peaceful alignment with everyone. Your thoughts are your own, and they can be treasure or trouble.

I invite you to be positive and do all you can with the expectation that God will help if you align with and invite the connection. If nothing else, personal connection with God can make a real difference in your Peace, Power, and Potential.

16 - Your Team Could Consider

The major challenge for your team may simply be to get created in the first place. I write from a different place than most articles and stories that I read.

My writing comes from possibilities in the future with the hope that better days can be attracted to the reality of every prisoner and every taxpayer. What we have is not working for anybody.

I invite you and your families to consider new potentials and then pray them and visualize them and conceptualize them in,to manifestation like a general contractor does a house. Prayer still works as does Visualization, Conceptualization, and Manifestation.

It is difficult to move these possibilities forward in the real world but the spiritual world has less obstacles and more possibilities. Could you spend more time in the spiritual world?

I invite you to create your teams, consider many areas of focus nd then work on Manifestation. Some things that I would like you to consider praying for, studying about and reporting about are:

Twitter-Like Spousal Script Messaging

E-cards to and From Prison Messaging

Twitter-Like Parent/Child Messaging

Twitter-Like Prisoner/Parent Script Messaging

Twitter-Like Prisoner/Sibling Script Messaging

Self-Support Community Messaging

Stigma Neutralization Messaging

Family Development Project Messaging

Going Back or Fresh Start Messaging

Anchor Point Messaging

Reality Check Messaging For Opportunity Niches

Well Read Prisoner Messaging

Messaging To Inner City Minors From Prisoners

Communications with Industry Opportunity Messaging

Tax Rewards For Hiring Ex-Prisoners Messaging

Chase Probabilities Not Fantasies Messaging

Positive Messaging About Interacting With Police

Strikes Against You Messaging

Care Taker Jobs

Seasonal Opportunities & Plan B's Messaging

Re-Earn Standing Messaging

Lifer's Spirit Messaging

How to Get Out Of Jail Legally Messaging

Getting Real Ready Messaging

Prison Nutrition Messaging

Messaging To The Politicians

For
Considering
These
Ideas

Ever

It Does Not Help Prayer Still Does!

19 - Resource Books

Distant Healing Sessions (or Join Mail List) – Write To mikewann@voicenet.com

Books by Rev. Mike at www.Amazon.com

Veterans Healing Six Pack
1. *Trauma Healing Options for VA Hospitals: Help for Veterans to Own Their Healing and their future.*
2. *Trauma Healing Action Steps for Veterans: Help to Start Healing*
3. *Trauma Healing Action Steps for Veterans: Empowerment*
4. *Trauma Healing Action Steps for Veterans: Forgiveness*
5. *Trauma Healing Action Steps for Veterans: Thought Freedom*
6. *Tea For Veterans: Welcome One Home*

PTSD Power Pack:
1. *The PTSD Project: Turn Pain To Power*
2. *PTSD & Soul Retrieval: Putting One Back Together*
3. *PTSD & The Purple PAD: Calling all Scientists and PTSD Patients*

Angel Raphael Speaks Volume 1: Take Courage! God Has Healing in Store for You!
Angel Raphael Speaks Volume 2: Take Courage! God Has Healing in Store for You!
Angel Raphael Speaks Volume 3: Take Courage! God Has Healing in Store for You!
Angel Raphael Speaks Volume 4: Angels, Addicts, Alcoholics & Prisoners – Oh Yeah!
Angel Raphael Speaks Volume 5: Prisoners Caring for Alcoholics - Australia In Miniature Projects Intro
Angel Raphael Speaks Volume 6: Prisoners Caring for Addicts - Australia In Miniature For Addicts
Reiki Journaling from Japan
Reiki Is Alive: God's Great Gift
Four Parts to Healing
Distant Healing: We Are All Connected
Stress Release Energy Work: How To Cope
Does Reiki Love Heal Cancer?
Group Consciousness
Salute To Philadelphia VA Medical Center: Thank You
Reiki Transcript for Reiki 2 & 3 Channels: Dr. Usui Is That You?
God Bless Kindle & Amazon
Puppies Are Different From People
If Your Dog Dies
Toy Guns Are Obsolete

Great Spirit Made Children With Red Skin: AND
The Cage of Fear: Is Not Locked
God Made Children Red, Yellow, Brown, Black & White: Greet Each Child With Kindness
Emergency Medical Kindness In The Cradle Of Liberty: Big City - Cracked Bell
Angels Are Always Around Addicts and Addicts: Help Is Near Now! Invite It In!
Angels Are Always Around Addicts and Alcoholics: Volume 2 - Tools To Help Re-Light Your Life
Prison Jobs Now: Providing Care For Addicts And Addicts
Controlled Care Communities Concept
Prison Possibilities Dialogue Series: Concept
Prison Possibilities Dialogue Series: Volume 2, 3, 4, 5 Dialogues
Prison Possibilities Voluntary Exile
Prison Possibilities Corrections Coaches
Prison Possibilities For Mexicans: Is A Boat Better Than A Wall?
Prison Possibilities Family Time: A Reason to Thrive!
Prison Genius Pool: "So Much Genius In Jail"
Prison Possibilities Access Control: Prisoner Access by Request
Prisoner's Lawyers Can Save The American Economy: Make A Buck Doing It & Be Thanked!
Prisoner Family Talks, Days, Stays & Vacations: Connecting Helps Healing
Prisoner Writing Projects: Write To Heal, Start Over & Reconnect
Prison Cell Clearing & Blessing: Clear Entities, Chase Ghosts, and & Create Sacred Space
Prisoner Professors: Show You Are Aware Create Change With Care
Prison Reiki? Maybe Someday? A Gateway To Help Heal Prisons & America?
Judges and An Angel Rule On Possibilities: We Can Cut Sentences & Prison Costs
Ideas For Prison Wardens: Leadership Is Not Easy
Solitary Community: Could Community Support Cut Costs and Issues?

Little Books at Kindle.com by Rev. Mike:
English Medical History Questionnaire For Non-English Speakers
English Language Helper For Non-English Speakers
Wise Wonderful Women Are The Well Of The Family
Answers for Test & Research: Dowsing Power
Crisis? Reiki! Baby? Reiki!
Bible References For Healing
Angel Raphael Speaks – Prisons
Angel Raphael Speaks – Veterans
The Saint Off Interstate 95

20 - Angels Please Prayers

Addict's

Angels of Healing Selected
Help Me to Stay Directed
Come To Me From The Sky
I Am Ready to Succeed Not Try
If I Don't Invite You In
I Might Not Win
I Have Been Lost For Too Long
Help Me To Stay Strong

Alcoholic's

Angels of Healing On High
Help Me to Stay Dry
Come To Me From The Sky
I Am Ready to Succeed Not Try
If I Don't Invite You In
I Might Not Win
I Have Been Lost For Too Long
Help Me To Stay Strong

From

21 - Private Channeling

Angel Raphael Speaks is a series of free messages that are channeled through Reverend Mike Wanner for the Highest good and Highest Healing of all concerned.

Many questions arise about Reverend Mike doing private channeling, and he does help with that so e-mail him.

Reverend Mike is available worldwide as a psychic channel, emotional release facilitator, spiritual energy practitioner & teacher, and public speaker. He looks forward to meeting you soon!

Email - mikewann@voicenet.com 215-342-1270 PRIVATE SPIRITUAL READINGS/channelings or Spiritual Healing Sessions: Telephone or in person. Rev. Mike is available for private, one-on-one intuitive sessions with you, his Guide Family, and your Guides. He helps by offering clarity on emotional situations about your life, your purpose, your spirituality, and the release of stuffed emotions and cellular memory.
Connect to the love of your Guides today!
Contact Rev. Mike for an appointment.
Sessions available:
Spiritual Readings
Angel Channeling
Distant Reiki Healing
Distant Clearing of Stuffed Emotions
Distant Clearing Cellular Memory
Distant Clearing Energy Blockages
Distant Clearing of the Chakras
Customized needs
Mastermind dowsing responses to yes/no direction finding questions.

Rev. Mike is a facilitator of healing. He invites you and the Divine to come together so that you can align with the Divine and have a great time and a great life. All healing is the one needing healing, and God unified, as it should be. Go ahead and start without Rev. Mike. Visit his prayer site http://www.Create-A-Prayer.com. Take the first step NOW.

22 - Reverend Mike Wanner

Rev. Mike Wanner started his metaphysical and ministerial studies with Reiki in 1993 and had studied seven styles of Reiki in the U.S., Japan, Canada, Denmark and Australia. He is certified to teach. He became certified to teach Integrated Energy Therapy in 1999 and co-taught the first IET class of the new Millennium. Mike began dowsing in 2001.

Ordained as a Metaphysical Minister of the International Metaphysical Ministry and an Interfaith Minister of the Circle of Miracles Ministry, Rev. Mike practices and teaches spiritual energy therapies in the Philadelphia Area.

Rev. Mike holds ministerial degrees from the University of Metaphysics and the University of Sedona. He is a Pastoral Care Associate of Aria - Frankford Hospital. He taught at the National Academy of Massage Therapy and Health Sciences.

Rev. Mike was a faculty member of the Medical Mission Sister's Center for Human Integration's School of Integrated Body/Mind Therapies in Fox Chase, Philadelphia, PA for twelve years.

Rev. Mike is licensed by the teaching of Intuitional Metaphysics to practice Spiritual Healing and Scientific Prayer. Mike is also a Prayer therapist.

Rev. Mike was elected in 2007 to the status of "Fellow of the American Institute of Stress."

In 2008, Rev. Mike became a practitioner of Coincidental Recognition as he incorporated the CoRe System into his spiritual healing practice.

In 2009, Rev. Mike trademarked a new healing process called Quantum Quatro! Subtle Energy System Support®.

In 2011, Rev. Mike joined the outreach program known as the Health Advantage Group.

In 2012, Rev. Mike became a Certified Professional Coach by The Master Coaching Academy and Joined the Personal Empowerment Group.

Before his metaphysical, ministerial and coaching studies, Rev. Mike worked for Sears Roebuck and Co. while in High School and after graduation, until he joined the U. S. Air Force in 1965. He returned to Sears from Vietnam in 1969 and stayed until 1978. His final Sears assignment was as an efficiency expert in Methods - Operational Research and Development.

He volunteered with Burholme Emergency Medical Services from 1969 and is still a Life Member and Board of Directors Member. He started a private ambulance company in 1975 and worked professionally in the field until 2001 when he devoted his full attention to real estate investing, healing, coaching, and writing.

www.ingramcontent.com/pod-product-compliance
Lightning Source LLC
Chambersburg PA
CBHW071201220526
45468CB00003B/1115